JUSTIN BIEBER

CANADIAN SINGER

MR VIVEK KUMAR PANDEY

Made with ♥ on the Notion Press Platform
www.notionpress.com

Contents

Foreword

During Writing This Book No Character No Religion Are Harmed It's Only For Study Purpose.We don't want to hurt anyone. In This Book There Is Short Biography Of Canadian Singer Justin Bieber & It's Life Style,Achievement,etc.

Preface

Author biography in English :

MY NAME IS VIVEK KUMAR PANDEY . I WAS BORN IN 30 SEP 2002,I AM FROM SURAT GUJARAT INDIA.MY DREAM WAS TO BE GOOD WRITERS ,MY FAMILY SUPPORTED ME TO SUCCESSFUL AND I CAN DO IT MY SELF.How do I write? That is a question, I believe, that can be honestly answered by me."CELEBRATING YOUNGEST WRITER AWARD WINNER IN GUJARAT 1ST RANK" MR PANDEY JI . I may think I did a good job writing something. The reader is the one who decides the quality of my writing. I do find writing to be natural to me and therefore find it to be a real challenge. My trick as a challenged writer is to do the best I can and know that I am happy with the final outcome. It may take a while to do my best and there may be quite a few problems I run into along the way.

I am not a greedy person those who are thinking about me and my self I never tried it anyone people suffering from sadness ,I trying to get promoted people suffering from happiness and joy in your Life Time. Now in current situation in India and also world people are unemployed and have no many but our indian governor help to people to get free food from ration card , i also take part in leadership team ,i am Motivational speaker , Film script writer. There was my two dream firstly writer and secondly actor & also my own film is upcoming soon i done almost completely completed script for my film .I AM GOING TO SAY WORD OF HEART TOUCH OUT PLEASE READ IT" , firstly i thanks my father he supports me in this field they always getting inspired me by own his words and behavior ,they always said that he was a biggest person in the world in future and also they purchase fruit and chocolate for me in anytime & anyway , firstly my father buy him then call me Vivek you want a chocolate i will say yes papa but how many tell me ,papa: you tell me how much i buy him i told 1 or 2 chocolate but my father purchase whole the boxes of chocolate and they get suprised me.

MY FATHER WAS BORN IN " 20 SEPTEMBER" 1971 IN INDIA.

1) MY FATHER FAVORITE CLOTHES IS KURTA PAIJMA AND ALSO STYLES SHOE

2) FAVORITE SINGER IS KISHORE DA

3) FAVORITE STATE GUJARAT AND KOLKATA , HIS VILLAGE IN BIHAR

4) FAVORITE COLOR BLACK AND WHITE

THEY ALSO LOVE cricket like IPL and one day t-20 .they also like watching a News daily and heard the song daily ,they also interested in tik tok video but in current time tik tok is banned in india but also few videos are in you tube. In lockdown time my family and me very enjoy day daily. my father play daily ludo with his sister and son, daughter.they always loved tea and coffee anytime call me ". I make it tea for my father but some reason after the April to june they are suffering from fever and cough , weakness on 6 June 2020 my father death. they not told me say bye bye his life. After death of 6 June on 10 june my mom and dad anniversary.but my father is Best in the world they can do anything for me please take care of father and respect it of your parents.

ONE
Justin Bieber

- **Justin Bieber**

1. During Writing This Book No Character No Religion Are Harmed It's Only For Study Purpose.We don't want to hurt anyone. In This Book There Is Short Biography Of Canadian Singer Justin Bieber & It's Life Style,Achievement,etc.

Justin Drew Bieber (born March 1, 1994) is a Canadian singer. Bieber is recognized for his genre-melding musicianship and has played an influential role in modern-day popular music. He was discovered by American record executive Scooter Braun and signed with RBMG Records in 2008, gaining recognition with the release of his debut seven-track EP My World (2009) and soon establishing himself as a teen idol.

Bieber achieved commercial success with his teen pop-driven debut studio album, My World 2.0 (2010), which debuted atop the US Billboard 200, making him the youngest solo male act to top the chart in 47 years. The album spawned the internationally successful single "Baby", which became one of the highest certified singles of all time in the US. His second studio album, Under the Mistletoe (2011), became the first Christmas album by a male artist to debut at number one in the US. Bieber experimented with dance-pop in his third studio album, Believe (2012), and went on to become the first artist in history with five US number-one albums at age 18. Between 2013 and 2014, Bieber was involved in multiple controversies and legal issues, which had a drastic impact on his public image.

In 2015, Bieber explored EDM with the release of "Where Are Ü Now", which won the Grammy Award for Best Dance/Electronic Recording. The song's musical direction played an instrumental role in his fourth studio album, Purpose, which produced three US number-one singles: "Love Yourself", "Sorry", and "What Do You Mean?". He became the first artist in history to occupy the entire top three of the UK Singles Chart. Bieber diversified on numerous collaborations between 2016 and 2017, including "I'm the One" and his remix to "Despacito" — both reaching number one on the US Billboard Hot 100 a week apart, making him the first artist in history to chart new number-one songs in consecutive weeks. "Despacito" was named the greatest Latin song of all time by Billboard and earned Bieber his career-first Latin Grammy Award. In 2019, he released a country collaboration with Dan + Shay, "10,000 Hours", which won the Grammy Award for Best Country Duo/Group Performance.

In 2020, Bieber released his R&B-led fifth studio album, Changes, which debuted at number one in both the UK and US, and a standalone duet with Ariana Grande, "Stuck with U", which debuted atop the US Billboard Hot 100. Bieber returned to his pop roots on his sixth studio album, Justice (2021). It produced the worldwide hit "Peaches" and debuted atop the US Billboard 200, making him the youngest soloist to have eight US number-one albums, a record held previously by Elvis Presley since 1965. The same year, Bieber released "Stay" with the Kid Laroi, which became his eighth US number-one single.

Bieber is one of the best-selling music artists of all time, with estimated sales of over 150 million records worldwide. He is credited with three Diamond certifications from the RIAA for "Baby", "Sorry" and "Despacito". He has received numerous accolades, including two Grammy Awards, one Latin Grammy Award, eight Juno Awards, two Brit Awards, one Bambi Award, 26 Billboard Music Awards, 18 American Music Awards, 22 MTV Europe Music Awards (the most wins for any artist), 23 Teen Choice Awards (the most wins for a male individual), and 33 Guinness World Records. Time named Bieber one of the 100 most influential people in the world in 2011, and he was included on Forbes' list of the top ten most powerful celebrities in 2011, 2012, and 2013.

He is the son of Jeremy Jack Bieber and Pattie Mallette, who were never married. Mallette's mother Diane and stepfather Bruce helped her raise her son. Bieber's ancestry includes French-Canadian, Irish, English, Scottish, and German.

Through his father, Jeremy, Bieber has three younger half-siblings. Jeremy and his ex-girlfriend, Erin Wagner, who broke up in 2014 after seven years together, have two children, daughter Jazmyn and son Jaxon. Jeremy married his girlfriend Chelsey in February 2018, and they have a daughter named Bay. Bieber also has a stepsister named Allie, the daughter of his stepmother. Pattie worked a series of low-paying office jobs, raising Bieber as a single mother in low-income housing. Bieber has maintained contact with his father.

Bieber attended a French-language immersion elementary school in Stratford, the Jeanne Sauvé Catholic School. He graduated from high school in Stratford, the St. Michael Catholic Secondary School, in 2012 with a 4.0 GPA. Growing up, he learned to play the piano, drums, guitar, and trumpet. In early 2007, aged 12, Bieber sang Ne-Yo's "So Sick" for a local singing competition in Stratford and was placed second. Mallette posted a video of the performance on YouTube for their family and friends to see. She continued to upload videos of Bieber singing covers of various R&B songs, and Bieber's popularity on the site grew. In the same year, Bieber busked shows in front of Avon Theatre steps with a rented guitar during tourism season.

- Justin Bieber at a signing event in 2009.

While searching for videos of a different singer, Scooter Braun, a former marketing executive of So So Def Recordings, clicked on one of Bieber's 2007 YouTube videos by accident. Impressed, Braun tracked down the theatre Bieber was performing at, located Bieber's school, and finally contacted his mother Mallette, who was initially reluctant because of Braun's Judaism. She remembered praying, "God, I gave him to you. You could send me a Christian man, a Christian label!", and, "God, you don't want this Jewish kid to be Justin's man, do you?" However, church elders convinced her to let Bieber go with Braun. At age 13, Bieber went to Atlanta, Georgia, with Braun to record demo tapes. Bieber began singing for Usher one week later.

Bieber was soon signed to Raymond Braun Media Group (RBMG), a joint venture between Braun and Usher. Justin Timberlake was reportedly also in the running to sign Bieber but lost the bidding war to Usher, partly due to the idea that two associated Justins would confuse the market.

Usher then sought assistance in finding a label home for the artist from then manager Chris Hicks, who helped engineer an audition with his contact L.A. Reid of The Island Def Jam Music Group. Reid signed Bieber to Island Records in October 2008 (resulting in a joint venture between RBMG and Island Records) and appointed Hicks as executive vice-president of Def Jam, where he could manage Bieber's career at the label. Bieber then moved to Atlanta with his mother to pursue further work with Braun and Usher. Braun became Bieber's manager in 2008.

Bieber's first single, "One Time", was released to radio while Bieber was still recording his debut album. The song reached number 12 on the Canadian Hot 100 during its first week of release in July 2009, and peaked at number 17 on the Billboard Hot 100 chart in the United States. During fall 2009, it had success in international markets. The song was certified platinum in Canada and the US and gold in Australia and New Zealand. His first release, an extended play titled My World, was released on November 17, 2009. The album's second single, "One Less Lonely Girl", and two promotional singles, "Love Me" and "Favorite Girl", were released exclusively on the iTunes Store and charted within the top 40 of the US Billboard Hot 100. As a result, he became the first solo artist to have four singles chart in the top 40 of the Hot 100 before the release of a debut album.

"One Less Lonely Girl" was later also released to radio and peaked within the top 20 in Canada and the US, and was certified gold in the latter. Following the release of My World, Bieber became the first artist to have seven songs from a debut album chart on the Billboard Hot 100. My World was eventually certified platinum in the US and double platinum in both Canada and the United Kingdom. To promote the album, Bieber performed on several live shows such as mtvU's VMA 09 Tour, European program The Dome, YTV's The Next Star, The Today Show, The Wendy Williams Show, Lopez Tonight, The Ellen DeGeneres Show, It's On with Alexa Chung, Good Morning America, Chelsea Lately, and BET's 106 & Park. Bieber also guest starred in an episode of True Jackson, VP in late 2009.

Bieber performed Ron Miller and Bryan Wells's "Someday at Christmas" for former US President Barack Obama and first lady Michelle Obama at the White House for Christmas in Washington, which aired on December 20, 2009, on US television broadcaster TNT. Bieber was also one of the performers for Dick Clark's New Year's Rockin' Eve with Ryan Seacrest, on December 31, 2009.

- Justin Bieber performing at the 2010 White House

Bieber was a presenter at the 52nd Annual Grammy Awards on January 31, 2010. He was invited to be a vocalist for the remake of the charity single "We Are the World" for its 25th anniversary to benefit Haiti after the earthquake. Bieber sings the opening line, which was sung by Lionel Richie in the original version.

On March 12, 2010, a version of K'naan's "Wavin' Flag", recorded by a collective of Canadian musicians known as Young Artists for Haiti, was released. Bieber is featured in the song, performing the closing lines.

In January 2010, "Baby" was released from his debut album My World 2.0. The song featured Ludacris, and became an international hit. It charted at number five on the US Billboard Hot 100, peaked at number three on the Canadian Hot 100 and reached the top ten in several international markets. Two promo singles, "Never Let You Go" and "U Smile", were top 30 hits on the US Hot 100, and top 20 hits in Canada. According to review aggregator Metacritic, the album has received generally favourable reviews. It debuted at number one on the US Billboard 200, making Bieber the youngest solo male act to top the chart since Stevie Wonder in 1963. My World 2.0 also debuted at number one on the Canadian Albums Chart, Irish Albums Chart, Australian Albums Chart, and the New Zealand Albums Chart and reached the top 10 of fifteen other countries.

To promote the album, Bieber appeared on several live programs including The View, the 2010 Kids' Choice Awards, Nightline, Late Show with David Letterman, The Dome and 106 & Park. Sean Kingston appeared on the album's next single "Eenie Meenie". The song reached the top ten in the United Kingdom and Australia, and the top 20 of most other markets. On April 10, 2010, Bieber was the musical guest on Saturday Night Live. On July 4, 2010, Bieber performed at the Macy's Fourth of July Fireworks Spectacular in New York City.

The following single from My World 2.0, "Somebody to Love", was released in April 2010, and a remix was released featuring Bieber's mentor Usher. On June 23, 2010, Bieber went on his first official headlining tour, the My World Tour, starting in Hartford, Connecticut, to promote My World and My World 2.0. In May 2010, Bieber featured in Soulja Boy's song "Rich Girl". In July 2010, it was reported that Bieber was the most searched-for celebrity on the Internet. That same month, his music video for "Baby" surpassed Lady Gaga's "Bad Romance" (2009) as the most viewed, and also the most disliked, YouTube video at the time. In September 2010, it was reported that Bieber accounted for 3% of all traffic on Twitter, according to an employee of the social-networking site.

- Justin Bieber performing in Indonesia

On My World 2.0, Bieber's voice was noted to be deeper than it was in his debut EP, due to puberty. In April 2010, the singer remarked regarding his vocals: "It cracks. Like every teenage boy, I'm dealing with it and I have the best vocal coach in the world ... Some of the notes I hit on "Baby" I can't hit any more. We have to lower the key when I sing live." Bieber guest-starred in the season premiere of the CBS American crime drama CSI: Crime Scene Investigation, which aired on September 23, 2010. He played a "troubled teen who is faced with a difficult decision regarding his only brother", who is also a serial bomber. Bieber was also in a subsequent episode of the series, which aired on February 17, 2011, in which his character is killed.

Bieber performed a medley of his singles "U Smile", "Baby", and "Somebody to Love", and briefly played the drums, at the 2010 MTV Video Music Awards on September 12, 2010. Bieber announced in October 2010 that he would be releasing an acoustic album, called My Worlds Acoustic. It was released on November 26, 2010, in the United States and featured acoustic versions of songs from his previous albums, and accompanied the release of a new song titled "Pray".

A 3-D part-biopic, part-concert film starring Bieber entitled Justin Bieber: Never Say Never, was released on February 11, 2011, directed by Step Up 3D director Jon M. Chu. It topped the box office with an estimated gross of $12.4 million on its opening day from 3,105 theatres.

It grossed $30.3 million for the weekend and was narrowly beaten by the romantic comedy Just Go with It, which grossed $31 million. Never Say Never reportedly exceeded industry expectations, nearly matching the $31.1 million grossed by Miley Cyrus's 2008 3-D concert film, Hannah Montana & Miley Cyrus: Best of Both Worlds Concert, which holds the record for the top debut for a music-documentary. Never Say Never grossed a total of $98,441,954 worldwide.

The film is accompanied by his second remix album, Never Say Never – The Remixes, released February 14, 2011, and features remixes of songs from his debut album, with guest appearances from Miley Cyrus, Chris Brown, and Kanye West, among others. One song from the album, "That Should Be Me", featuring country music band Rascal Flatts, won him his first award in country music for Collaborative Video of the Year at the CMT Music Awards in June 2011. Time magazine named Bieber one of the 100 most influential people in the world on their annual list. In June 2011, Bieber was ranked No. 2 on the Forbes list of Best-Paid Celebrities under 30. He is the youngest star, and 1 of 7 musicians on the list, having raked in $53 million in a 12-month period. The same month, his collaborative single "Next to You" with American singer Chris Brown has released. The unfinished video for that song was leaked online on June 6, and the official video was released on June 17.

On November 1, 2011, Bieber released the Christmas-themed Under the Mistletoe, his second studio album. It became the first Christmas album by a male artist to debut at No. 1 on the Billboard 200, and sold 210,000 copies in its first week of release. On November 19, 2021, the album was listed among the Greatest of All Time Top Holiday Albums chart by Billboard. The first single from the album, "Mistletoe" peaked at number one on the US Billboard Holiday 100 and Holiday Digital Songs charts. Bieber released "All I Want for Christmas Is You (SuperFestive!)" as the second single from the album, which is a re-recorded version of Mariah Carey's original single "All I Want for Christmas Is You" with Carey providing vocals on the track. Billboard listed the album and its singles, among the greatest Holiday albums and songs of all time, respectively.

- Justin Bieber at the 2012 NRJ Music Awards

In late 2011, Bieber began recording his third studio album, titled Believe. The following week, Bieber appeared on The Ellen DeGeneres Show to announce that the first single would be called "Boyfriend", and was released on March 26, 2012. The song debuted at number two on the US Billboard Hot 100, selling a total of 521,000 digital units, the second-highest-ever debut digital sales week.

Bill Werde of Billboard noted that it failed to debut at number one because the digital download of the track was available only through the iTunes Store, "restricting the buying option for those do not frequent the Apple retail store". "Boyfriend" became Bieber's first single ever to reach the top position on the Canadian Hot 100 by debuting at number one and staying on for one week. Bieber was featured on American hip hop group Far East Movement's song "Live My Life", from their fourth studio album Dirty Bass, in February 2012. The song emerged online five days before its scheduled release date and peaked within the top 30 of the Billboard Hot 100.

The first promotional single from the album, "Die in Your Arms", was released on May 29, 2012, and the second promotional single, "All Around the World" featuring American rapper Ludacris, followed the next week. The second single from Believe, "As Long as You Love Me" featuring rapper Big Sean, was released on June 11, 2012. It peaked at number six on the Billboard Hot 100.

His third studio album, Believe, was released on June 19, 2012, by Island Records. The album marked a musical departure from the teen pop sound of his previous releases, and incorporated elements of dance-pop and R&B genres. Intent on developing a more "mature" sound, Bieber collaborated with a wide range of urban producers for the release as well as some long-time collaborators, including Darkchild, Hit-Boy, Diplo, and Max Martin. Entertainment Weekly praised Bieber's musical shift, calling the album both a "reinvention and a reintroduction".

Rolling Stone noted the deeper voice and more "intense" beats found on the album, although it lampooned one of his euphemisms for newfound sexual maturity ("If you spread your wings, you can fly away with me"). Believe debuted at number one on the Billboard 200, becoming his fourth number-one album.The album sold 57,000 copies in its first week in Canada, debuting atop the Canadian Albums Chart. In September 2012, Bieber was featured on

"Beautiful", a song from Carly Rae Jepsen's second studio album, Kiss (2012).In October 2012, the third single from Believe, "Beauty and a Beat" featuring rapper Nicki Minaj, was released. The music video held the record for the most video views in 24 hours when it was released, with 10.6 million views.

- Justin Bieber performing during his Believe

The Believe Tour, which further promoted the album, began in September 2012 in Glendale, Arizona. On December 14, 2012, Bieber appeared on The Ellen DeGeneres Show, where he announced plans to release an acoustic album titled Believe Acoustic, which was released on January 29, 2013.

Bieber returned to Saturday Night Live as the host and musical guest on the February 9, 2013 episode. His appearance was panned by critics and cast members, including Kate McKinnon, who said Bieber was not comfortable with his hosting duties, and Bill Hader, who said he did not enjoy the presence of Bieber or his entourage. Hader added that in his eight years on the television program, Bieber was the only host who lived up to his reputation.

On March 7, 2013, Bieber fainted backstage at London's O2 Arena after complaining of breathing problems throughout his concert performance and was taken to the hospital. Bieber cancelled his second Lisbon, Portugal concert at the Pavilhão Atlântico, which was to be held on March 12, because of low ticket sales. The concert held in the same venue on March 11 did go on as scheduled.

In mid-August 2013, a remixed duet version of Michael Jackson's previously unreleased song "Slave to the Rhythm", featuring Bieber, leaked online. In response to criticism over this remix, the Michael Jackson Estate stated that it had not authorized the release of this recording, and has since made attempts to remove the song from as many web sites and YouTube channels as possible. Later, a song titled "Twerk" by rapper Lil Twist, featuring Bieber as well as Miley Cyrus, also leaked. In September, Bieber was featured in Maejor Ali's song "Lolly" with rapper Juicy J. A music video for "Melodies", the debut single of American singer Madison Beer, was released in the same month featuring Bieber in a cameo appearance.

On October 3, 2013, Bieber announced that he would release a new song every Monday for 10 weeks as a lead-up to the film Justin Bieber's Believe, which entered production in May 2012 and was released on December 25, 2013. The film is a follow-up to Bieber's first theatrical film Justin Bieber: Never Say Never, with Jon M. Chu returning as director. The first song of Music Mondays, "Heartbreaker", was released on October 7. The second song, "All That Matters", was released on October 14, followed by "Hold Tight" on October 21, "Recovery" on October 28, "Bad Day" on November 4, and "All Bad" on November 11.

The seventh song, "PYD" featuring R. Kelly, was released on November 18; it was followed by "Roller Coaster" on November 25, and "Change Me" on December 2. The final song, "Confident" featuring Chance the Rapper, was released on December 9, 2013. That same day, it was announced that all 10 tracks will be featured on an upcoming collection called Journals. It reportedly featured five additional unreleased songs, a music video for "All That Matters", and a trailer for Believe. Journals was only available for purchase via iTunes for a limited time only: from December 23, 2013, to January 9, 2014. The titles of the five new additional songs are: "One Life", "Backpack" featuring Lil Wayne, "What's Hatnin' " featuring Future, "Swap It Out", and "Memphis" featuring Big Sean and Diplo. Bieber released a song titled "Home to Mama" featuring Australian singer Cody Simpson in November 2014. The same month, Bieber topped Forbes magazine's Forbes 30 Under 30 annual ranking, which lists the highest-earning celebrities under 30 for that year.

Because of the disbanding of Universal Music's division, The Island Def Jam Music Group, in April 2014, Bieber and a number of artists were subsequently transferred to another Universal Music-related division, Def Jam Recordings, causing Bieber to no longer be signed to Island Records.

- Justin Bieber and his manager Scooter Braun

In February 2015, Bieber released "Where Are Ü Now", a collaboration with Jack Ü. The song peaked at number eight on the Billboard Hot 100 and reached number one on Billboard's Hot Dance/Electronic Songs chart. It earned Bieber his career-first Grammy Award for Best Dance/Electronic Recording at the 58th Annual Grammy Awards. In March 2015, Bieber made an appearance in the music video for Carly Rae Jepsen's single "I Really Like You".

In March 2015, Bieber was the featured roastee in Comedy Central's annual roast special, and was a contestant on the reality competition series Lip Sync Battle. Bieber filmed an episode for the Fox TV reality series Knock Knock Live, and aired before the show was cancelled after two episodes. On August 28, 2015, Bieber released a new single titled "What Do You Mean?" as the lead single from his fourth studio album Purpose. The song is a blend of teen pop, electronic dance music and acoustic R&B.

It debuted at number one on the US Billboard Hot 100 and became Bieber's first number-one single in the country. He set a Guinness World Record by becoming the youngest solo male artist to debut at the top of the Hot 100. It also broke the record for the fastest song to reach number one on US iTunes, reaching the top spot in under 5 minutes.

On October 23, 2015, Bieber released the album's second single titled "Sorry", which debuted at number two on the Billboard Hot 100. After eight non-consecutive weeks at number two, on the week charting January 23, 2016, "Sorry" climbed to the top of the chart and became Bieber's second number-one single on the Billboard Hot 100. The third single from Purpose, "Love Yourself" also peaked at number one in the US, making Bieber the first male artist in almost a decade to have three number-ones from an album since Justin Timberlake, who did it previously with his album FutureSex/LoveSounds in 2006–07.

He also became the first solo artist to chart three solo songs in the top five of the Billboard Hot 100 simultaneously, and the first as a lead act since the Beatles in 1964. "Love Yourself" topped Billboard's Year-End Hot 100 chart in 2016, followed by "Sorry" at number two, and made Bieber only the third artist in history to hold the top-two positions of the Billboard Year-End Hot 100, after the Beatles in 1964 and Usher in 2004. An album track on Purpose, "Company", was announced as the fourth single on March 8, 2016. On February 12, 2016, Bieber's first four albums were released on vinyl for the first time.

On January 8, 2016, Bieber made UK chart history by becoming the first artist to occupy the entire top three of the UK Singles Chart. He achieved this feat as "Love Yourself", "Sorry" and "What Do You Mean?" charted at positions 1, 2 and 3 simultaneously. On July 22, 2016, Bieber released a new single with EDM trio Major Lazer and Danish singer Mo titled "Cold Water". It debuted at number two on the Billboard Hot 100, becoming Bieber's third number-two debut on the ranking, passing Mariah Carey's record to become the artist with the most number-two debuts in the US.

In August 2016, Bieber was featured on French DJ DJ Snake's single "Let Me Love You". The song peaked at number four on the Billboard Hot 100. Bieber was also featured on American singer Post Malone's single "Deja Vu", which later appeared as the fourth single from the latter's debut studio album Stoney in September 2016. Bieber then appeared in the documentary Bodyguards: Secret Lives from the Watchtower (2016). At the 59th Annual Grammy Awards, Purpose was nominated for Album of the Year and Best Pop Vocal Album, whereas "Love Yourself" received nominations for Song of the Year and Best Pop Solo Performance respectively. Bieber was the headlining act at the 2016 iHeartRadio Jingle Ball and gave a closing performance on December 9, 2016.

On April 17, 2017, Puerto Rican singers Luis Fonsi and Daddy Yankee released a remix for their song "Despacito" featuring Bieber. It was the first song by Bieber in which he sings in Spanish. The remix became a worldwide success and broke major chart records around the world. The song reached number one in the US and joined "Macarena" (1996) as the only English/Spanish songs to reach number one on the Billboard Hot 100.

It tied the then-record for the most weeks at number one in Billboard Hot 100 history. The song spent a record 56 weeks at number one on Billboard's Hot Latin Songs chart and broke the then-record for most weeks at number one on the Digital Songs Sales chart. The remix is the most viewed song of all time on the crowdsourced media knowledge base Genius, with 23.3 million views. The song earned Bieber his first career Latin Grammy. As of September 2021, "Despacito" holds the number-one position on the Greatest of All Time Hot Latin Songs chart and number-five on the Greatest of All Time Songs of the Summer chart by Billboard.

Bieber, along with rappers Quavo, Chance the Rapper, and Lil Wayne, provided vocals on DJ Khaled's single "I'm the One", released on April 28, 2017. The song debuted at number one on the Billboard Hot 100, becoming Bieber's second number-one debut and his fourth song to top the chart. One week later, "Despacito" topped the charts in the US, which became his fifth number-one single and made Bieber the first artist in history to notch new No. 1s in back-to-back weeks. "I'm the One" also reached number one on Billboard's Hot Rap Songs and Hot R&B/Hip-Hop Songs charts. On June 9, 2017, French DJ David Guetta released "2U", in which Bieber was featured. The first music video for "2U" features Victoria's Secret models lip synching to the song.

On August 17, 2017, Bieber released the single "Friends" with American record producer and songwriter BloodPop. Songwriters Julia Michaels and Justin Tranter, having previously worked with him on "Sorry" in 2015. At the 60th Annual Grammy Awards, "Despacito" received three nominations for Record of the Year, Song of the Year, and Best Pop Duo/Group Performance respectively. Bieber did not attend the show to perform the nominated song, claiming that he would not make any award show appearances until his next album was finished. In July 2018, Bieber reunited with DJ Khaled in "No Brainer", co-featuring again with Chance the

Rapper and Quavo. The single peaked in the top five of the Hot 100 and reached number one on Billboard's Hot R&B Songs chart. He was also featured in the accompanying music video.

On April 21, 2019, Bieber delivered a surprise performance at the 2019 Coachella music festival, marking his first live performance in two years, and teased his return to music with a new album. On May 10, 2019, British singer Ed Sheeran and Bieber released the single "I Don't Care", from Sheeran's album No.6 Collaborations Project (2019). The pair had previously collaborated, with Sheeran co-writing Bieber's 2015 song "Love Yourself", and 2016 song "Cold Water" with Major Lazer. "I Don't Care" became a worldwide hit, reaching number-one in 26 countries, while peaking at number two in the United States.

Bieber later featured on a remix of Billie Eilish's breakthrough single "Bad Guy", which was released on July 11. On October 4, 2019, Bieber and country music duo Dan + Shay released the song "10,000 Hours", which peaked at number four on the US Billboard Hot 100. It became the highest-charting non-holiday country song in the history of the Billboard Streaming Songs chart and spent 21 weeks at number one on Billboard's Hot Country Songs chart. As a result, Bieber became the first act in history to reach number one on seven multi-metric charts: Hot 100, Hot Country Songs, Hot Dance/Electronic Songs, Hot Latin Songs, Hot R&B Songs, Hot R&B/Hip-Hop Songs, and Hot Rap Songs. It earned Bieber his second Grammy Award for Best Country Duo/Group Performance at the 63rd Annual Grammy Awards. On October 14 2019, Bieber became the youngest solo male artist to spend 200 cumulative weeks in the top 10 of the Billboard Hot 100.

- Justin Bieber announced

On December 24, 2019, Bieber announced that he would be releasing his fifth studio album and embarking on his fourth concert tour in 2020. The album's first single, "Yummy", was released on January 3, 2020. It debuted at number two on the

Billboard Hot 100. On December 31, 2019, Bieber also released a trailer announcing his 10-part YouTube Originals docu-series Justin Bieber: Seasons, which focused on an array of themes: his life post-hiatus from music, marriage, preparation for new music, and battle against Lyme disease. Episodes were released weekly on Mondays and Wednesdays from January 27, 2020.

The docu-series amassed 32.65 million views within its first week of release, breaking the all-time record for the most-viewed premiere in its first week of all YouTube Originals. Appearing on The Ellen DeGeneres Show on January 28, 2020, Bieber finally confirmed the release date of his fifth studio album, Changes, to be February 14, 2020. The same day, he also released a promotional single for the album, "Get Me", featuring American singer-songwriter Kehlani. On February 7, 2020, Bieber released "Intentions" featuring Quavo, as the second single from the album. The song peaked at number five on the Billboard Hot 100. Changes was released on February 14, debuting at number one on the UK and US Billboard 200 charts, making Bieber the youngest solo artist in history to have seven number-one albums in the US.

On May 8, 2020, American singer Ariana Grande and Bieber released the single "Stuck with U", to help raise funds for the first responders of the COVID-19 pandemic and their families. The song debuted atop the Billboard Hot 100, becoming his sixth number-one single in the US. On September 4, 2020, Bieber played a lead starring role in the music video for DJ Khaled's single "Popstar" featuring Drake.On September 18, 2020, Bieber released a collaboration with Chance the Rapper titled "Holy", which Bieber called the start of his new era and the first single from his upcoming sixth studio album. It peaked at number three on the Billboard Hot 100.

On October 15, 2020, he released "Lonely", a collaboration with Benny Blanco as the second single from his upcoming album. The song peaked at number 12 on the Billboard Hot 100. Bieber and J Balvin were featured on a remix of 24kGoldn's single, "Mood", which was released on November 6, 2020. On November 20, 2020, Shawn Mendes and Bieber released "Monster", for Mendes' fourth studio album, Wonder. It peaked at number eight on the Billboard Hot 100.

On January 1, 2021, Bieber released the third single "Anyone" from his upcoming studio album, which peaked at number six on the Billboard Hot 100. On February 14, 2021, Bieber performed "Journals Live" in collaboration with TikTok, which marked his first-ever performance of his 2013 album Journals. It became the first long-form concert event on the platform and broke the record for the most-viewed single-artist livestream in the platform's history. On February 26, 2021, Bieber officially announced that his sixth studio album would be titled Justice. On March 5, 2021, Bieber released the album's fourth single, "Hold On", which peaked at number 20 on the Billboard Hot 100.

Justice and its fifth single, "Peaches", were both released on March 19, 2021, and met with generally positive reviews. It debuted at number one on the Billboard 200, becoming Bieber's eighth number-one project, while "Peaches" debuted at number one on the Billboard Hot 100, becoming his seventh number-one single respectively. As a result, Bieber set major records in the US. Bieber became the youngest solo artist to have eight US number-one albums, breaking a 56-year-old record held by Elvis Presley. He became the first solo male artist in history to simultaneously debut a song and an album at number one in the US. He also became the first male act to have his first 6 studio albums debut at number one on the Billboard 200.

On Easter 2021, Bieber surprise-released Freedom, a gospel-inspired EP consisting of six songs. On April 11, 2021, Justice led the Billboard 200 by less than 1,000 units, and became Bieber's first full-length album to spend more than one week at the top of the chart in over a decade. On May 10, 2021, Bieber was co-featured on DJ Khaled's "Let It Go", with 21 Savage. He also starred in the accompanying music video. He was also featured on the song "What You See" from Migos' fourth studio album Culture III. On July 9, 2021, Bieber released a collaboration with the Kid Laroi titled "Stay".

The song debuted at number three on the Billboard Hot 100. It later peaked at number one in its fourth week on the chart, becoming his eighth number-one single in the US. "Stay" also became his 100th career entry on the chart, making him the youngest solo artist to chart 100 songs on the Billboard Hot 100, a record later broken by American rapper Lil Baby. It also became the first song by a male foreign act to achieve a Perfect All-Kill in South Korea. "Stay" was the most-streamed song globally on Apple Music in 2022. Bieber was the headlining act for the "Freedom Experience" show at the SoFi Stadium as part of 1DayLA's COVID-19 service event, held on July 24, 2021.

On August 13, 2021, Bieber released a remix to Nigerian singer Wizkid's song "Essence", his career-first song in afrobeats. It elevated the song's position to number nine on the Billboard Hot 100. A week later, he released a collaboration with Skrillex and Don Toliver titled "Don't Go". On September 4, 2021, Bieber headlined the 2021 Made in America Festival held at the Benjamin Franklin Parkway in Philadelphia. On October 8, 2021, Bieber released a new documentary film titled Justin Bieber: Our World to give viewers an inside-view in preparation for his 2020 "New Year's Eve Live" powered by T-Mobile, his first concert performance in three years.

On October 29, 2021, he released "Rockin' Around the Christmas Tree", a cover of Brenda Lee's holiday classic, on streaming platforms worldwide. On November 15, 2021, Bieber announced the international legs of his upcoming fourth concert tour, the Justice World Tour, scheduled to begin in San Diego, California on February 18, 2022. On November 19, 2021, Bryson Tiller released the single "Lonely Christmas" with Bieber co-featured alongside his long-time collaborator Poo Bear. On December 3, 2021, Bieber released a collaboration with American rapper Juice Wrld titled "Wandered to LA" as the second single from the rapper's second posthumous album Fighting Demons. Bieber was the headlining performer at the 2021 Saudi Arabian Grand Prix held on December 5, 2021, in Jeddah, Saudi Arabia. On December 11, 2021, he headlined the 2021 Jingle Bell Ball held by Capital FM at The O2, London. The same month, Justice received 8 nominations at the 64th Annual Grammy Awards.

- Justin Bieber Musical style

During the early years of his career, Bieber often spoke about his admiration for Michael Jackson (left), as well as his influence on him.Bieber's music is mainly pop, and occasionally dance-pop or EDM. In 2010, Jody Rosen of Rolling Stone asserted that the content of his music was "offering a gentle introduction to the mysteries and heartaches of adolescence: songs flushed with romance but notably free of sex itself". During the initial years of his career, his musical style was noted for being aimed to a more teen pop and "bubblegum-ish" direction.

In January 2012, Bieber told V magazine: "I want to do it at my own pace. I don't want to start singing about things like sex, drugs and swearing. I'm into love, and maybe I'll get more into making love when I'm older. But I want to be someone who is respected by everybody."

- Justin Bieber Voice

Bieber initially sang with a boy soprano voice, before his voice broke, as was evidenced during the debut performance of "Pray" at the 2010 American Music Awards. Sean Michaels of The Guardian described puberty as "the biggest threat to his career" at the time. Jody Rosen commented that Bieber sings with "swing and rhythmic dexterity" on his debut album, noting his tone to be "nasal".

Bieber started to receive voice coaching from Jan Smith in 2008.As an adult singer, Bieber's voice type is tenor, with a vocal range spanning from the baritone A2 to the high tenor F5. In a review of his Purpose album, Neil McCormick of The Daily Telegraph complimented his "soft, supple and seductive singing". Caroline Sullivan of The Guardian also praised Bieber's "affectedly breathy voice", noting that "the voice soon palls, but the songs are often interesting."

- Justin Bieber Business ventures and endorsements

In 2010, Bieber signed a deal with Proactiv. In the same year, Bieber partnered with Nicole by OPI to launch a nail polish line "The One Less Lonely Girl Collection", which sold exclusively in Walmart. Bieber's nail polish line sold one million bottles less than two months after its release. Bieber endorsed Adidas, beside Derrick Rose and Venus Williams, in 2012. He became the new "face" and "body" of Calvin Klein in early 2015. Entertainment Tonight reported that Bieber had used MYO-X, a dietary supplement, in preparation for the photo shoot. In June 2015, Bieber teamed up with StarShop, a new shopping app launched by Kevin Harrington. Bieber endorses Beats By Dre, Elizabeth Arden and Best Buy. Bieber has been credited with boosting the careers of other singers such as Carly Rae Jepsen and Madison Beer when he tweeted about them.

Bieber has released four fragrances. He launched his debut fragrance, Someday, in 2011. it grossed more than three million US dollars in sales, at Macy's, in just under three weeks, which industry experts regard as a successful celebrity-led launch. On the heels of that 2011 best-seller, he launched his second fragrance, Girlfriend, in June 2012. His third fragrance, The Key, was launched in July 2013, and his latest fragrance, Justin Bieber Collector's Edition, launched in 2014.

In January 2019, Bieber launched his own clothing line called "Drew House", consisting of a wide range of products. Most products feature the brand's defining symbol of a simple yellow smiley-face logo with the text "drew" written across the front. Bieber trademarked the name for his company in February 2018. In September 2019, after a year-long collaboration with Schmidt's Naturals CEO, Michael Cammarata, Bieber released his deodorant line, "Here + Now", designed for sensitive skin. In October 2020, Bieber collaborated with Crocs on a limited edition of the brand's renowned clogs called "Crocs x Justin Bieber". The design draws on Crocs' classic clog range with inputs of purple and yellow, inspired by Bieber's personal clothing brand, Drew House. The limited edition clogs sold at select Crocs and partner e-commerce channels, Drew House's website, and Crocs retail stores in China and South

Korea.

In fall 2021, Bieber collaborated with Tim Hortons to launch a specialty version of Timbits known as "timbiebs". CNN credited the promotion's role in contributing to an increase in Tim Hortons' sales by 10.3% in the fourth quarter of 2021. On February 7, 2022, Bieber starred in Balenciaga's first 2022 campaign alongside Kim Kardashian and Isabelle Huppert. In April 2022, Italian brand Vespa revealed its collaboration with a new limited edition of its famed scooter curated by Bieber. The "JUSTIN BIEBER X VESPA" is modelled on a Piaggio Sprint base – available in 50, 100 and 100cc guise. In May 2022, Bieber and Tim Hortons partnered once again in a new collaboration called the "Biebs Brew", a French vanilla cold brew, which was available in North American stores beginning June 6, 2022.

In December 2022, Bieber launched a clean water technology company called "Generosity" that aims to provide sustainable drinking water by reducing the usage of single-serve plastic. Alongside Micah Cravalho, he showcased 150 water fountains at the 2022 FIFA World Cup held in Qatar. Generosity fountains dispense refillable alkaline water after connecting to a water source, and are expected to be commercially available at major venues and homes in 2023.

- Justin Bieber performing in Zürich in 2011

Usher commented that while he and Bieber were both signed at the same age, "I had the chance to ramp up my success, where this has happened to Bieber abruptly". As a result, when he was younger, Usher, Braun, Bieber's bodyguard, and other adults surrounding Bieber constantly coached him on handling fame and his public image. After signing Bieber, Usher appointed one of his former assistants, Ryan Good, to be Bieber's road manager and stylist. Good, once nicknamed Bieber's "swagger coach", created a "streetwise look" for the singer which consisted of baseball caps, hoodies, dog chains, and flashy sneakers. Amy Kaufman of The Los Angeles

Times comments, "Though a product of a middle-class suburban upbringing in Stratford, Ontario, Bieber's manner of dress and speech suggest he's mimicking his favourite rappers.

" In 2013, Bieber said he was "very influenced by black culture", but he neither thought "of it as black or white" nor tried to "act or pose in a certain way". To him, it was "a lifestyle—like a suaveness or a swag". Bieber was often featured in teen magazines such as Tiger Beat, and has been labelled a "teen heartthrob". In 2010, he was frequently criticized for looking and sounding younger than his age, and the following year for an androgynous appearance, which had been commonly noted in the media, including his appearance on the cover of LOVE magazine's androgyny issue in 2011.

His signature wings hairstyle at the time brought much attention in particular. His teen-pop music, image (especially as a heartthrob to girls), and the media attention he receives have additionally been criticized. He has been a target of Internet bloggers and message board posters, especially users of the Internet message board 4chan and of YouTube. Nick Collins of The Daily Telegraph said that "Bieber's character appears to strike a particularly sour note with his Internet critics" who have questioned his manner of speech, among other things.

- Justin Bieber(left) wearing ripped jeans

During 2013–2014, Bieber's teen heartthrob and clean-cut image was drastically threatened due to several controversial events surrounding him. Notable controversies during this period include him abandoning his pet monkey in Germany; vomiting onstage, being videoed by his friend as he urinated in a bucket and yelled “Fuck Bill Clinton”; wearing a gas mask in public; being involved in an explicit image with a stripper; and allegedly assaulting his bodyguard and a limo driver. Bieber's uncle, Brad Bieber, said that his troublesome behaviour was caused by his break up with Selena Gomez. In its March 2014 edition, Rolling Stone put Bieber on its cover alongside the title 'Bad Boy'. In the same year, Bieber claimed to have changed his name to simply "Bizzle". During the "Bizzle" phase, Bieber donned a quiff and often wore thick gold chains and baseball caps.

In his early 20s, especially after the release of Purpose in 2015, Bieber's public image changed again — in a more positive light as he was involved in less controversy. He notably had bleached blond hair and often wore rock branded t-shirts; including Marilyn Manson and Kurt Cobain t-shirts; flannel shirts, denim jackets and ripped jeans. He also wore kilts, a trend of 1990s fashion, on several occasions. Vogue remarked that his fashion during this period was reminiscent of grunge fashion during the 1990s. After his marriage in 2018, Bieber's persona continued to change. As his fan base got older and he got married, he transitioned away from the teenage heartthrob image, taking on a more mature personality and a more soft-spoken style of speech. In an interview with Vogue in February 2019, Bieber said that he would "laugh at his past self".

Wax statues of Bieber with the hairstyle from his early career are on display at the Madame Tussauds wax museums in New York City, London, and Amsterdam. In 2018, "Steps to Stardom", an exhibit on Bieber's early career, opened in his hometown of Stratford, Ontario at the Stratford Perth Museum, offering a collection of mementoes from his formative years and rise to international stardom. The items on display include a professional drum kit he owned as a younger child, his Grammy Award, microphones, his Stratford Warriors hockey jacket, and personal letters, including one from Michelle Obama. Bieber made a number of visits to the museum. "Steps to Stardom" was originally scheduled to close in October 2018 but the board of the museum extended its stay for at least another year after the exhibit broke attendance records set by its Anne Frank House exhibit in 2015.

In 2011, at age 17 and within just two years of his professional music career, Bieber was named amongst the Time 100 world's most influential people list and was ranked number 2 on the Forbes Highest-Paid Celebrities Under 30 list. He went on to be included on the Forbes annual list five more times; in 2012, 2013, 2014, 2016 and

2017.

- Justin Bieber YouTube and Twitter Account

"Beliebers" gathering around the hotel where Bieber is supposed to be inside in Oslo, Norway in May 2012.Bieber's early fanbase developed on YouTube and predated the release of his debut album My World. According to Jan Hoffman of The New York Times, part of Bieber's appeal stems from his YouTube channel. Chicago Tribune noted that Bieber's fanbase, "Beliebers", was among the top words of 2010. Long before the release of My World in November 2009, his YouTube videos attracted millions of views.

Braun recognized the appeal. Before flying him to Atlanta, Braun wanted to "build him up more on YouTube first" and had Bieber record more home videos for the channel. "I said: 'Justin, sing like there's no one in the room. But let's not use expensive cameras.' We'll give it to kids, let them do the work, so that they feel like it's theirs", recalled Braun. Bieber continues to upload videos to the same channel and has opened a Twitter account, from which he interacts with fans regularly. In January 2013, Bieber surpassed Lady Gaga as the most-followed person on Twitter for the first time and held the record for 11 months.

As of 2022, Bieber is the third-most-followed user on Twitter and the most-followed musician on the platform, with over 113 million followers. His YouTube channel is currently the most viewed music channel for an individual on the platform, having attracted over 29 billion views. With over 70 million subscribers, he remains the most subscribed solo artist on YouTube and held the overall record for six years. A record-tying 11 music videos by Bieber have surpassed over 1 billion views on YouTube, his most recent being "Beauty and a Beat". The music video for Bieber's song "Baby" is among the most liked videos on YouTube, having received over 22 million likes since its upload in 2010. Bieber was frequently a trending topic on Twitter when the feature first launched, as his fans frequently discussed him on the network, and was named the top-trending star on

Twitter in 2010.

- Justin Bieber Personal life

As Bieber resides in the United States, he is reported to possess an O-1 visa for temporary resident status, based on "extraordinary ability or achievement" in a field. Bieber has said he is not interested in obtaining US citizenship, and has praised Canada as being "the best country in the world", citing its mostly government-funded health care system as a model example. However, in September 2018, TMZ reported that Bieber had begun the process of becoming an American citizen, following his marriage to Hailey Baldwin. Bieber owns a $25.8 million home in Beverly Hills as well as a lakeside home in Ontario.

- Justin Bieber Relationships

Bieber's father, Jeremy Bieber, is a former carpenter and pro-am mixed martial artist. In March 2014, Rolling Stone characterized Jeremy as having "split with Justin's mom when Justin was a toddler, and wasn't always around afterward. But he has, as of late, accepted a place of honor in his superstar son's entourage".

From 2008 to 2009, Bieber was in a relationship with Caitlin Beadles; the two remained friends, and Beadles attended Bieber's wedding. From December 2010 to March 2018, Bieber was in an on-again, off-again relationship with singer and actress Selena Gomez. In an interview on The Ellen DeGeneres Show, Bieber stated that some of his songs including "Sorry", "Mark My Words", and "What Do You Mean?" are about his relationship with Gomez. From August to December 2016, he was linked to model Sofia Richie.

Bieber became engaged to model Hailey Baldwin on July 7, 2018. They had briefly dated from December 2015 to January 2016 before splitting, then reconciled in June 2018. Bieber and Baldwin reportedly obtained a marriage license in September 2018, leading to reports that they had a civil marriage. On September 14, 2018,

Baldwin stated on Twitter that she and Bieber had not yet married, but deleted the tweet afterward. On November 23, 2018, Bieber stated he was married to Baldwin. Bieber and Baldwin had an official ceremony in Bluffton, South Carolina, on September 30, 2019.

- Justin Bieber Beliefs

Bieber has described himself as a faithful Christian, said he communicates with God via prayer, and that "He's the reason I'm here". He reflected his faith in a music video with Brandon Burke, titled "#iPledge", in which he talks about God's forgiveness. Bieber was baptized on January 9, 2014, by Pentecostal pastor Carl Lentz of Hillsong Church, New York, after a born again experience. He has described Lentz as a good friend. However, following allegations of abuse about Lentz from his former nanny, Bieber stated Hillsong is "not his church" and that he was now a part of Churchome.

When asked how he wants to raise his children, Bieber said, "I'm a Jesus follower. When you accept Jesus, you walk with the Holy Spirit. I just want to be led by the Holy Spirit." Many of Bieber's tattoos have religious significance including the medium-sized cross on his chest and a tiny cross under his eye. Bieber also covered up the "Son of God" text tattooed on his abdomen with a large design that features two angels, gothic arches, a skeleton and a serpent. On July 24, 2021, Bieber led worship with Gospel singers Kari Jobe and Cody Carnes during the "Freedom Experience" at SoFi Stadium.

The trio performed "The Blessing".Regarding sexual abstinence, Bieber told music magazine Rolling Stone in 2011, "I don't think you should have sex with anyone unless you love them." He added that he does not "believe in abortion", and that it is "like killing a baby". When asked about the case of abortion with regard to rape, however, he said, "I guess I haven't been in that position, so I wouldn't be able to judge that." However, in 2022, amidst Roe v. Wade being overturned, both Bieber and his wife expressed disapproval, with Bieber posting on his Instagram story stating "For what it's worth, I think women should have the choice what to do with their own bodies." His view on sexual orientation is quoted as "everyone's own decision", and he has contributed to the It Gets Better Project, a non-profit group aiming to prevent suicide among LGBT youth.

Bieber supports Pencils of Promise, a charity founded by Adam Braun, the younger brother of Bieber's manager. The organization builds schools in developing countries, and Bieber became manager for the organization's campaign in Guatemala. He serves as a celebrity spokesman for the organization by running ads for the charity and its campaign "Schools4All". He promises to visit schools that donate the most funds to the organization. He takes part in the charity's fund-raising galas and donates parts of the proceeds from his concerts and Someday line of fragrances, and various merchandising to the charity. In 2010, Bieber supported a campaign for People for the Ethical Treatment of Animals (PETA) by urging fans to adopt abandoned pets from shelters.

Bieber donated his hair to Ellen DeGeneres during his appearance in her talkshow The Ellen DeGeneres Show in March 2011. His hair sold on eBay for more than $40,000 and the proceeds benefited the animal rescue charity, The Gentle Barn. Following the earthquake and tsunami in Japan in March 2011, Bieber donated proceeds from his concerts in Japan to Japanese Red Cross in May 2011. In December 2011, Bieber donated $100,000 to Whitney Elementary School in Las Vegas to provide students from low income families. Bieber supported Charity: Water, a nonprofit that brings potable drinking water to people in developing countries. On his birthday in 2011 and 2012, he launched his campaign to urge his followers to donate on Twitter. Bieber was named top charitable celeb of 2011 by American news aggregator and blog HuffPost.

In 2013, Bieber launched his online #GiveBackPhilippines campaign for helping the victims of Typhoon Haiyan and travelled to the Philippines after raising $3 million. His work in the country earned him a star on the Philippine Walk of Fame. He also supports Children's Miracle Network Hospitals and Alzheimer's Association.

In September 2017, Bieber donated $25,000 to the American Red Cross to help people in Texas after the severe destruction caused by Hurricane Harvey.

On February 7, 2020, Bieber donated $100,000 to Julie Coker, a 22-year-old fan who works in mental health awareness. Coker revealed that her own past struggles with mental health motivated her to work for mental health. She praised Bieber by saying," has a big following, so if he has a good message about mental health, hopefully everybody else ... will want to start thinking about mental health in a different way."

In February 2020, Bieber made a donation to Beijing Chunmiao Children Aid Foundation in China to support COVID-19 relief.Bieber and Ariana Grande collaborated on the single "Stuck With U", released in May 2020 as the first of series of singles coordinated by entertainment executive Scooter Braun, who is also Bieber's manager, to support the COVID-19 pandemic. All net proceeds from the song went to the First Responders Children's Foundation to fund grants and scholarships for children of first responders and health care workers who worked on the front lines during the pandemic. By August 2021, the single had raised over $3,500,000. In September 2020, Bieber and Chance the Rapper announced that they've partnered with Cash App and will donate $250,000 to fans who are struggling during the pandemic.

In March 2021, Bieber visited the California State Prison in Los Angeles County along with his wife Hailey and pastor Judah Smith at the invitation of Scott Budnick. Bieber met with inmates involved in The Urban Ministry Institute and expressed support for Budnick's Anti-Recidivism Coalition. During the visit, Bieber committed to provide buses to transport relatives of the inmates who have been unable to see them due to the COVID-19 pandemic in California.Bieber described his visit to the prison as a "life-changing experience that I will never forget".

- Justin Bieber Legal issues and controversies

Bieber had several run-ins with the law around the world before his first arrest in 2014, including when he was accused of reckless driving in his neighbourhood in 2012, and charged in Brazil with vandalism in 2013. One of his neighbours in Calabasas, California, accused Bieber of throwing eggs at his home on January 9, 2014, and causing thousands of dollars of damage.

On January 23, 2014, Bieber was arrested in Miami Beach, Florida, together with singer Khalil, on suspicion of driving under the influence (DUI), driving with an over six month expired license, and resisting arrest without violence. Police said that Bieber told authorities he had consumed alcohol, smoked marijuana, and taken prescription drugs. He was released from these charges on a $2,500 bond. A toxicology report revealed that Bieber had THC and the anti-anxiety medication Xanax in his system at the time of his arrest. However, in January 2021, he reflected on this event, describing it as "not finest hour" and encouraging fans to "let the forgiveness of Jesus take over and watch your life blossom into all that God has designed you to be."

- Justin Bieber mugshots taken on January 23

Following Bieber's arrest on the DUI charge, more than 270,000 people petitioned the White House seeking to have him deported from the United States. Although the number of signatures received was sufficient to require a response under published White House guidelines, the Obama Administration declined substantive comment on the petition.Immigration Law expert Harlan York noted that the likelihood of Bieber being deported was extremely slim. York stated, "About a decade ago, the Supreme Court ruled that driving under the influence, typically, is not a basis to deport someone."

In April 2013, Bieber was criticized for writing a message in the guestbook at the Anne Frank House which read, "Truly inspiring to be able to come here. Anne was a great girl. Hopefully she would have been a belieber." After the message was posted on the museum's Facebook page, Bieber received widespread criticism on social media for perceived insensitivity and narcissism. The Anne Frank House defended Bieber, stating, "He's 19. It's a crazy life he's living, he didn't mean bad He was very interested in the story of Anne Frank and stayed for over an hour. We hope that his visit will inspire his fans to learn more about her life and hopefully read the diary."

On July 9, 2014, Bieber was charged with one misdemeanour count of vandalism in California for throwing eggs at his Calabasas neighbour's home in January. Police earlier claimed that they had video footage of him high-fiving friends after the eggs were thrown. With him pleading no contest to the charge, the Los Angeles County Superior Court sentenced him on July 9 to pay $80,900 in restitution, serve two years' probation, complete 12 weeks of anger management, and five days of community service in what the district attorney termed a negotiated settlement. Since then, he has permanently moved to Beverly Hills, California.

On August 13, 2014, the January DUI case was settled with a plea bargain; Bieber pleaded guilty to resisting an officer without violence and a lesser charge of driving without due care and attention. He was fined US$500 and sentenced to attend a 12-hour anger management course and a program that teaches the impact of drunken driving on victims. As part of the plea bargain, he made a US$50,000 contribution to Our Kids, a local children's charity.

On September 1, 2014, Bieber was arrested and charged with assault and dangerous driving near his hometown of Stratford, Ontario, after a collision between a minivan and Bieber's all-terrain vehicle on August 29. Ontario police said that he then "engaged in a physical altercation" with an occupant of the minivan. He was released shortly and his lawyer blamed the incident on "the unwelcome presence of paparazzi".On September 8, Toronto dropped an assault charge against him originally brought up on January 29 for an incident with a limousine driver in December 2013. In November 2014, he was ordered to appear in Argentina within 60 days by a Buenos Aires court to give testimony on an alleged assault on a photographer on November 9, 2013. When he failed to do so, an arrest warrant was issued and two of his bodyguards were released in Argentina in April 2015.

I didn't want to come off arrogant or conceited, or basically how I've been acting the past year, year and a half ... although what's happened in the past has happened, I just want to ... be kind and loving and gentle and soft.

- Justin Bieber reflects in a video posted in January 2015

In June 2014, a video emerged of a 15-year-old Bieber telling a joke about black people, which used the word "nigger" multiple times. In the same month, a second video showed a 15-year-old Bieber giggling as he croons his song "One Less Lonely Girl", but parodying the main lyric as "One less lonely nigger", and stating that if he were to kill one, he would be "part of the KKK". He apologized the day the latter was released: "Facing my mistakes from years ago has been one of the hardest things I've ever dealt with."

In July 2017, the Chinese government banned Bieber from performing in China. A Chinese Bieber fan contacted the Beijing Municipal Bureau of Culture requesting the reason for the ban. The Bureau released a statement, explaining "Justin Bieber is a gifted singer, but he is also a controversial young foreign singer", and "In order to maintain order in the Chinese market and purify the Chinese performance environment, it is not suitable to bring in badly behaved entertainers." In 2021, Chinese streaming sites Youku, iQIYI, and Tencent Video removed Bieber's scenes in Friends: The Reunion donning Ross Geller's iconic "Spudnik" costume.

In June 2020, Bieber was accused of sexual assault by an anonymous woman, merely known as "Danielle", who claimed on Twitter that the singer had made non-consensual sexual acts at a Four Seasons hotel in Austin, Texas in March 2014 while with then-girlfriend Selena Gomez. The woman claimed that she had been inspired to tell her story by Twitter user 'itsgabby', who had accused actor Ansel Elgort of sexual assault the week prior. In a series of tweets Bieber denied all the allegations, stating that sexual abuse "is something I don't take lightly". He provided proof that he was not present in the location within the time that the alleged incident took place, dismissing all allegations. On March 23, 2022, Bieber dropped the $20 million lawsuit against the two Twitter users.

- Justin Bieber Health

Bieber has struggled with mental health issues, particularly depression and anxiety, at various points during his career. He has generally been open about these issues. In his American YouTube docu-series Seasons, the singer opened up about his struggles with addiction with frequent consumption of lean, pills such as MDMA, and hallucinogenic mushrooms in early stages of his career.

In January 2020, Bieber announced on his Instagram that he had been diagnosed with Lyme disease. He also revealed that he had infectious mononucleosis, which affected his neurological and overall health.

In February 2022, it was reported that Bieber had tested positive for COVID-19, two days after embarking on his fourth concert tour, Justice World Tour. In June of the same year, Bieber announced that he had been diagnosed with Ramsay Hunt syndrome type 2 and that half of his face was paralyzed. He canceled and postponed concerts and appearances due to the condition, but returned to live performances in late July.

In September, two days after the first concert in Latin America as part of the Rock in Rio festival, it was announced that all remaining dates of the tour would be suspended due to Bieber prioritizing his health. In a statement shared on social media, the singer said that "After getting off stage, the exhaustion overtook me and I realized that I need to make my health the priority right now. So I'm going to take a break from touring for the time being. I'm going to be OK, but I need time to rest and get better."

Bieber greeted by the US chairman of the Joint Chiefs of Staff, Mike Mullen, in 2011. Bieber is one of Canada's most successful musical exponents.Bieber has enjoyed pop stardom for over a decade and has been referred to as the "Prince of Pop" and the "King of Teen Pop" by contemporary journalists. Highlighting his longevity, he was awarded the MTV Award for Best New Artist in 2010 and the MTV Award for Artist of the Year in 2021. Rolling Stone India referred to him as the "biggest popstar of our age", "one of the most captivating artists of the century" and "one of the world's most successful artists of all time".

Bieber is often cited as a pop icon, or simply an icon. In a 2011 article comparing the cultural significance of Bieber to Facebook founder Mark Zuckerberg, the Orlando Sentinel said that, "Out of all the cultural icons who influence and inspire today's society, Justin Bieber is without a doubt one of the most prominent." He is generally credited as an important figure of the relationship between social media and music, which rose to prominence in the late 2000s; Variety dubbed him "a once-in-a-generation superstar who charted a swift and stunning rise from precocious YouTube talent to global phenomenon."

In an article titled 'How Justin Bieber revolutionised careers in the music industry' by The Guardian, Tom Fazakerley says that Social media has transformed the way people, brands and musicians communicate. The likes of MySpace and even more so YouTube, have enabled budding artists to put their music out to a massive audience at the click of a finger. This has taken down the barriers to the music industry and reshaped the career path for budding artists Nowadays you can be your own artist, producer and promoter - and if you do this well, like Justin Bieber, you can really make it.

At age 15, following the release of his 2009 singles "One Time" and "One Less Lonely Girl", Bieber's immediate popularity led him to appear on the likes of The Ellen DeGeneres Show, The Wendy Williams Show and Good Morning America. He had achieved a global fandom whom came to be known as "beliebers" and his popularity was labelled "Bieber Fever",with fan frenzies taking place in Liverpool, Barcelona and Paris, among other territories. Notably, it was revealed in 2020 that renowned singer Billie Eilish was nearly sent to therapy by her mother Maggie Baird due to her "obsession" with Bieber. Bieber's intense fandom was considered to be reminiscent of "Beatlemania", and his signature wings hairstyle at the time also drew comparisons to the Beatles' mop top hairstyle. Bieber's adoration from teenage girls was also likened to those of Frank Sinatra in the 1940s and Elvis Presley in the 1950s.

He's the only person in humanity who's grown up the way he has – with smartphones and cameras on him 24/7 ... Another kid can go out and have a good night on the town, and no one gives a crap, but Justin is the most Googled person on the planet – for four years straight!

- Justin Bieber maintained his global popularity

Bieber maintained his global popularity during his transition to adulthood, achieving increased artistic recognition and credit in the process. In respect to Bieber's success as a teenager to a young adult, Variety said that Bieber is arguably the first mega pop star to come of age entirely in the social media era and also called him an "Internet icon".

The Conversation's Jo Adetunji said that Bieber is "one of the most successful pop singers of recent years".Regarding his EDM-driven album Purpose (2015), which reached beyond the moment and trends of that period according to Adetunji, Adetunji argued that Bieber should be considered a serious creative artist. Adetunji compared the album to Madonna's Ray of Light (1998), Alanis Morissette's Jagged Little Pill (1995) and Justin Timberlake's FutureSex/LoveSounds (2006). Hugh McIntyre of Forbes said about Bieber that, "You may love him, you may hate him, but no matter how you feel about him, nobody can argue that Justin Bieber hasn't conquered the pop world The Grammy winner can turn essentially any track into a smash, and nobody can sell a single like he can these days." Also calling Bieber "an unstoppable force in music", McIntyre lauded Bieber for achieving success in various genres, including R&B, electronic dance, hip hop and Latin.

At age 19, Bieber received the fan-voted special Milestone Award at the 2013 Billboard Music Awards in recognition for being a creative artist who broke boundaries with his contribution to the musical landscape at the time, beating the likes of Taylor Swift and Bruno Mars to the award.

Bieber and his work have influenced various recording artists including Shawn Mendes, Why Don't We, Johnny Orlando, and Niall Horan.Singers Dua Lipa and Charlie Puth have stated that they were influenced by the discovery of Bieber on YouTube which inspired them to achieve the same.

- Justin Bieber Achievements

Throughout his career, Bieber has sold an estimated 150 million records worldwide, making him one of the best-selling music artists of all time. In 2011, Bieber was honoured with a star in front of Avon Theater in Stratford, Ontario, Canada, where he used to busk when he was younger. On November 23, 2012, Bieber was presented with the Queen Elizabeth II Diamond Jubilee Medal by the former Prime Minister of Canada, Stephen Harper. He was one of 60,000 Canadians to receive the Diamond Jubilee medal that year. In 2013, Bieber received a Diamond award from the Recording Industry Association of America (RIAA) for his single "Baby", which at the time became the highest-certified digital single of all time.

Bieber is credited with three Diamond Certified singles from the RIAA for "Baby", "Sorry", and "Despacito". Bieber has won two Grammy Awards out of 23 nominations, one Latin Grammy Award, eight Juno Awards, two Brit Awards, 26 Billboard Music Awards, and numerous fan voted accolades which include 18 American Music Awards, 23 Teen Choice Awards (the most wins for a male individual), eight iHeartRadio Music Awards, and six MTV Video Music Awards. He has also won a record 22 MTV Europe Music

Awards out of a record 52 nominations (the most for any artist).All of Bieber's studio albums are certified Platinum or higher by the RIAA and have received numerous accolades. He is the youngest (27) solo artist to have eight US number-one albums, a record held by Elvis Presley since 1965. Bieber is the first artist to have 10 songs surpass 1 billion streams each in Spotify history.

Following the release of his fourth studio album Purpose, Bieber set major milestones globally. He became the first artist, since Elvis Presley in 2005, to replace his own song as number one on the UK Singles Chart. He is the first artist in history to occupy the entire top three of the UK Singles Chart. He achieved this feat as "Love Yourself", "Sorry" and "What Do You Mean?" charted at positions 1, 2 and 3 simultaneously.The singles also peaked at number one in the US, making Bieber the first male artist since Justin Timberlake in 2007 to have three number-ones from an album.

He also became the first solo artist to chart three solo songs in the top five of the US Billboard Hot 100 simultaneously, and the first as a lead act since the Beatles in 1964. "Love Yourself" topped Billboard's Year-End Hot 100 Chart in 2016, followed by "Sorry" at number two, and made Bieber only the third artist in history to hold the top-two positions of the Billboard Year-End Hot 100, after the Beatles in 1964 and Usher in 2004. As of 2021, Bieber has set 33 Guinness World Records, which include eight that were achieved from the success of his album Purpose and was featured in the 2017 Edition. These records included the most streamed track on Spotify in one week, the most streamed album on Spotify in one week, the most simultaneous tracks on the US Billboard Hot 100, and the most simultaneous new entries on the US Billboard Hot 100 by a solo artist, among others.

Bieber has attained notable success on numerous Billboard charts both in the United States and globally. Eight singles by Bieber have topped the US Billboard Hot 100, his most recent being "Stay". He is the first artist in history to chart new number-one singles in consecutive weeks on the Hot 100. He is the youngest (21) male soloist to debut at number one in the US. He is also the youngest (25) male soloist to spend 200 cumulative weeks in the top 10 of the Hot 100. He is the first male soloist to simultaneously debut a song and an album at number one in the US.

He is also the first male soloist to spend 59 consecutive weeks in the top 10 of the Hot 100. Bieber is the first artist in history to reach number one on seven multi-metric Billboard charts: Hot 100, Hot Country Songs, Hot Dance/Electronic Songs, Hot Latin Songs, Hot R&B Songs, Hot R&B/Hip-Hop Songs, and Hot Rap Songs.His hit single "Despacito" has spent the most weeks at number one (56) on Billboard's Hot Latin Songs Chart and is ranked as the greatest Latin song of all time by Billboard.

He is the artist with the most number-one debuts (10), most number-one singles (13), and the most cumulative weeks at number one (56) on the Billboard Canadian Hot 100 Chart. Bieber is the solo artist with the most cumulative weeks at number one (163) on the Billboard Social 50 Chart. He was named the number one artist on Billboard's Decade-End Social 50 Chart for the 2010s. Bieber was named the "Greatest Pop Star of 2016" by Billboard. He was also Billboard's Year-End Top Male Artist for 2016 and placed number seven on the magazine's Decade-End Top Artists Chart for the 2010s. The magazine also ranked him 55th on the Greatest of All Time Artists and 38th on the Greatest of All Time Hot 100 Artists Charts respectively.

9 798889 091226

Printed by Libri Plureos GmbH in Hamburg,
Germany